EVERYTHING
BIRDS OF PREY

NATIONAL
GEOGRAPHIC
KiDS

EVERYTHING
BIRDS OF PREY

BLAKE HOENA

With National Geographic Explorer HILLARY S. YOUNG

CONTENTS

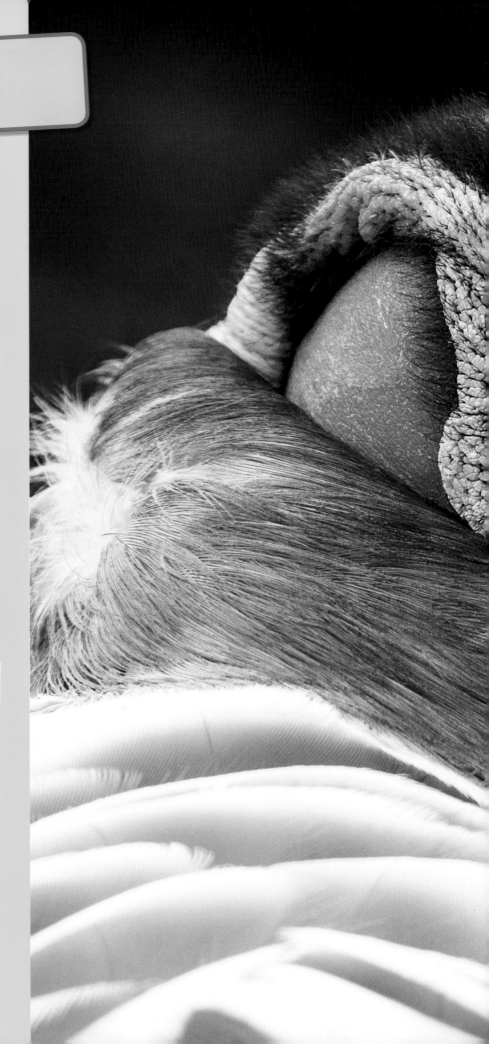

Introduction 6

1 MEET THE BIRDS OF PREY 8
What Is a Bird of Prey? 10
Who's Who 12
All Over the World 14
Superpowered Birds of Prey 16
A PHOTOGRAPHIC DIAGRAM:
Beak to Tail 18

2 RAPTOR LIFE 20
Nest Sweet Nest 22
Something's Hatching! 24
Bird Sense 26
On the Hunt 28
A PHOTO GALLERY:
Pick a Favorite! 30

3 BIRDS OF A FEATHER 32
Eyes on the Skies 34
A Bird in the Hand 36
Raptors and Robins 38
Raptor Report 40
RAPTOR COMPARISONS:
You vs. a Bird of Prey 42

4 FUN WITH BIRDS OF PREY 44
Fly Like an Eagle 46
A Little Bird Told Me 48
What's Your Bird of Prey-sonality? 50
Birds of Prey in Culture 52
PHOTO FINISH:
Behind the Shot With Hillary S. Young 54

AFTERWORD:
Top Predator, Top Ecologist 56
AN INTERACTIVE GLOSSARY:
Bird Words 60
Find Out More 62
Index 63
Credits 64

The king vulture is native to Central and South America and is known for its colorful bald head and fleshy wattle on its beak. Bird scientists don't know why its head is so colorful.

The Steller's sea-eagle's white upper wings and brown body make it easy to spot.

INTRODUCTION

LOOK UP! SEE THAT
WINGED FIGURE SOARING OVERHEAD?

No, it's not a plane. It's not a superhero either. It's a bird of prey. Birds of prey possess abilities that seem beyond natural. Falcons are the fastest animals alive. They are also agile enough to dart around like jet fighters as they snatch up insects and other birds to eat. Hawks have incredibly keen vision, and while hundreds of feet above the ground, they can spot mice scampering around in the grass below. Stealthy owls sneak up on unsuspecting prey by flying silently through the night, and eagles have razor-sharp talons powerful enough to crunch bones.

Whether you see an osprey circling overhead or a hawk swooping down from great heights, it's hard not to stop and stare in amazement. Birds of prey are some of the fastest and the largest flying animals in the world. Read on to learn EVERYTHING about these mighty hunters.

EXPLORER'S CORNER

Hi! I'm Hillary S. Young and I am an ecologist. I study the communities of animals that live in ecosystems all over the world, and how humans—yes, us—impact these communities. I often study birds because they are so sensitive to human impact and also so important to the functioning of our planet. Over my many years of research, I have had some fantastic experiences with birds of prey. Look for these Explorer's Corner boxes perched on pages throughout this book, where I will share stories of my research on bird behavior, habits, and habitat with you.

Griffon vultures feast on the carcass of a wild animal. Vultures are scavengers that feed on dead animals.

MEET THE
BIRDS OF PREY

WHAT IS A BIRD OF PREY?

SIMPLY PUT, A BIRD OF PREY
IS A LARGE, FLYING CARNIVORE, OR MEAT-EATER.

Birds of prey are skillful hunters, smart scavengers, and master fliers. They are fast and deadly when they go in for the kill, yet graceful as they slowly circle above searching for prey.

BIRDS OF PREY ARE ALSO CALLED RAPTORS, WHICH COMES FROM THE LATIN WORD RAPERE, MEANING "TO SNATCH OR CARRY OFF."

MICRORAPTOR

DINOS VS. BIRDS

Paleontologists, the scientists who study ancient life-forms, argue that birds descended from a group of dinosaurs called theropods. These dinos included the savage *Tyrannosaurus rex,* but also the smaller *Velociraptor* and the birdlike *Archaeopteryx.*

Don't believe it? Check out these similarities:

- Scientists say that theropods, especially young ones, had feathers to help them stay warm.
- Dinos like *Microraptor* even had feathery wings. And while no dinosaur could fly, some could glide and would swoop down from tall trees to attack prey, much like some modern-day raptors.
- *Deinonychus* had razor-sharp claws on its back feet, similar to a bird of prey's talons.
- Dinos and birds have scales—just check a bird's feet if you need proof.
- Like birds, dinos laid eggs.

Imagine a *T. rex* with wings! Luckily for us, birds of prey are only like mini–flying dinosaurs.

RAPTOR RAP FEATHERS MAKE BIRDS UNIQUE FROM ALL OTHER ANIMALS.

WHAT'S NOT A BIRD OF PREY?

Birds of prey aren't the only birds that eat other animals. Penguins dive into the water to chase after fish. Storks snag frogs with their long, pointy bills. Swallows dart after insects. But none of these are birds of prey. Why? They don't have all three of the specific features that separate birds of prey from their other feathery cousins:

- Sharp talons for snatching up prey
- Hooked beaks for tearing flesh
- Excellent vision to spy prey from far away

SOMETHING ROTTEN AND SMELLY

Just because they're carnivorous doesn't mean that birds of prey eat only live animals. Vultures and buzzards are known for eating carrion, or dead animal flesh. Eagles are very opportunistic eaters, and are as likely to snatch live fish out of the water as they are to eat dead fish that have washed up on shore. Snacking on dead animals takes a lot less energy than trying to hunt and kill live ones—somewhat like it being easier to buy cookies at the grocery store than it is to bake them yourself.

The scaly claws of a bird of prey look almost prehistoric.

By the Numbers

10,000 bird species live on Earth

450 bird of prey species live throughout the world

240 species are in the hawk family

150 species are in the owl families

WHO'S WHO

WHEN MOST PEOPLE THINK OF BIRDS OF PREY, THEY SIMPLY PICTURE

hawks and eagles, but these two types of raptors represent only one group. There are actually several hundred species of birds of prey, which include falcons, kites, owls, vultures—YES, vultures—kestrels, harriers, and more. These birds are divided into several groups based on their unique traits.

DAY HUNTERS

Falconiformes rely heavily on their excellent vision to find food and are diurnal, meaning they hunt during the day. There are five families of Falconiformes and each includes many species.

FAMILY ACCIPITRIDAE—includes hawks, kites, eagles, harriers, Old World vultures, and buzzards. There are about 240 species in this family.

FAMILY CATHARTIDAE—includes the seven species of New World vultures. What ties these birds together as a family are their bald heads, wide wing structures built for circling ominously overhead, and the fact that they feed mostly on carrion.

FAMILY FALCONIDAE—includes approximately 60 species. They are speedy and agile birds, and they need to be as they tend to hunt other flying critters. This fact is probably why they are unique in using their beaks to kill prey while in flight. They will snatch a bird out of the air with their talons and then quickly stab it with their beaks—trying to fly with another animal flapping its wings can be pretty dangerous!

FAMILY PANDIONIDAE—made up of ospreys. What sets these fish-eating birds apart from other diurnal birds is their feet. Their outer front toes can swivel backward to help them grasp on to the slippery fish that they prey on.

FAMILY SAGITTARIIDAE—made up of only secretary birds. They have long legs, which look more like a crane's than those of other birds of prey. They also have short toes and stubby talons. And even though they can fly, they spend much of their time on the ground hunting for insects and lizards.

BIRDS OF AN ORDER

All birds have some things in common, including feathers and wings. They also are vertebrates, or have backbones, and belong to a scientific class or group called Aves. But the bird family is so big that ornithologists, the scientists who study birds, have broken it down into groups called orders. Each order may include one or more families, and families can have many different species.

FAMILY ACCIPITRIDAE
HAWK

FAMILY CATHARTIDAE
VULTURE

FAMILY FALCONIDAE
FALCON

FAMILY SAGITTARIIDAE
SECRETARY BIRD

FAMILY PANDIONIDAE
OSPREY

RAPTOR RAP BEARDED VULTURES SOMETIMES KNOCK PREY OFF CLIFFS.

ORIENTAL BAY OWL

TWILIGHT AND NIGHT HUNTERS

Owls belong to the Strigiformes order, and they are separated from diurnal birds of prey largely because they are nocturnal. Well, mostly. Some are twilight owls who take advantage of the dusk hours between daylight and darkness to hunt. But it's more than just when a bird hunts that makes it an owl. Compare a picture of a typical hawk to a great horned owl and there are some obvious differences in the way they look. There are two families of Strigiformes.

FAMILY STRIGIDAE—is the larger of the two owl families, with up to 160 species. The majority of these owls live in temperate to tropic forest regions, so they don't usually migrate. Species include:

- Scops-owls
- Screech-owls
- Burrowing owls

FAMILY TYTONIDAE—includes about 16 species, of which the barn owl is the most common. They live all over the world and are mostly found in wooded areas. Species include:

- Barn owls
- Masked owls
- Bay owls

OWL VS. OWL

How do you tell owl from owl? With a little practice, it's easier than you think. Here are a few helpful pointers to help you eyeball members of the different Strigiformes families.

TEAM STRIGIDAE

1. **TWO ROUND FACIAL DISKS AROUND THEIR EYES**
2. **A LONG THIRD TOE WITH A SMOOTH CLAW**
3. **FOUR NOTCHES IN THEIR STERNUM**
4. **LARGER EYES**
5. **SHORT BEAKS**

SCREECH-OWL

TEAM TYTONIDAE

1. **HEART-SHAPED FACES**
2. **A PECTINATE CLAW, OR CLAW WITH A SERRATED EDGE, BELIEVED TO BE USED FOR CLEANING FEATHERS**
3. **TWO NOTCHES IN THEIR STERNUM**
4. **SMALLER EYES**
5. **THIN, ELONGATED BEAKS**

BARN OWL

ALL OVER THE WORLD

BIRDS OF PREY
LIVE ON EVERY CONTINENT, except for bitterly cold Antarctica—but can you blame them? And throughout the world, they are admired for their strength and hunting prowess. Because of these traits, many nations have even given birds of prey the honor of being their countries' national birds.

EXPLORER'S CORNER

While the 450 species of birds of prey found around the world have lots of shared traits, they also are amazingly varied even within one location. For example, the Philippine eagle is the largest eagle in the world in terms of length, and it needs lush, intact forests to hunt monkeys. The Philippine falconet, which lives in nearly the same location, is about the size of a sparrow and nests in old woodpecker holes in secondary forests. While the Philippine falconet is doing well, the Philippine eagle has suffered from forest loss, and there are fewer than 500 birds alive today. Remember, although all birds of prey are fierce and powerful hunters, in some parts of the world they need a little help and protection from us.

BALD EAGLE
The bald eagle is found throughout most of North America, north of the Mexico–United States border. Large, majestic birds, with stark white head feathers, they have been adopted as the United States' national bird.

NORTHERN CRESTED CARACARA
Mexico's national bird, northern crested caracaras are one of the oddest-looking birds of prey, with purple (juveniles) to bright orange coloring on their faces.

NORTH AMERICA

UNITED STATES

MEXICO

PANAMA   COLOMBIA

EQUATOR

ECUADOR

HARPY EAGLE
The largest eagle found in Central America, the harpy eagle is the national bird of Panama. They are also mighty hunters of the Amazon rain forest.

SOUTH AMERICA

CHILE

ANDEAN CONDOR
These New World vultures are among the largest birds of prey. They range up and down the Andes Mountains, so no wonder they are the national bird of South American countries such as Ecuador, Chile, and Colombia.

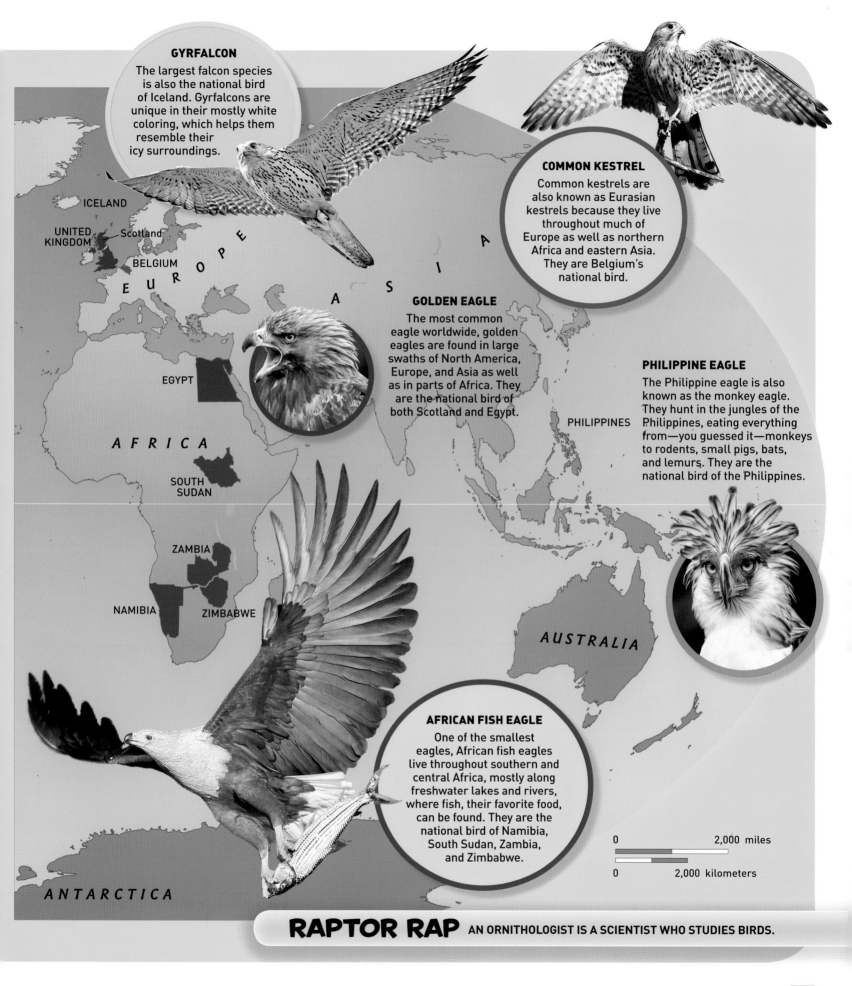

GYRFALCON

The largest falcon species is also the national bird of Iceland. Gyrfalcons are unique in their mostly white coloring, which helps them resemble their icy surroundings.

COMMON KESTREL

Common kestrels are also known as Eurasian kestrels because they live throughout much of Europe as well as northern Africa and eastern Asia. They are Belgium's national bird.

GOLDEN EAGLE

The most common eagle worldwide, golden eagles are found in large swaths of North America, Europe, and Asia as well as in parts of Africa. They are the national bird of both Scotland and Egypt.

PHILIPPINE EAGLE

The Philippine eagle is also known as the monkey eagle. They hunt in the jungles of the Philippines, eating everything from—you guessed it—monkeys to rodents, small pigs, bats, and lemurs. They are the national bird of the Philippines.

AFRICAN FISH EAGLE

One of the smallest eagles, African fish eagles live throughout southern and central Africa, mostly along freshwater lakes and rivers, where fish, their favorite food, can be found. They are the national bird of Namibia, South Sudan, Zambia, and Zimbabwe.

ICELAND

UNITED KINGDOM · Scotland

BELGIUM

E U R O P E

A S I A

EGYPT

A F R I C A

SOUTH SUDAN

ZAMBIA

NAMIBIA · ZIMBABWE

PHILIPPINES

AUSTRALIA

ANTARCTICA

| 0 | | 2,000 miles |
| 0 | | 2,000 kilometers |

RAPTOR RAP AN ORNITHOLOGIST IS A SCIENTIST WHO STUDIES BIRDS.

SUPERPOWERED BIRDS OF PREY

IF YOU'RE STILL NOT WOWED BY BIRDS OF PREY, YOU soon will be. Check out these amazing raptors. They highlight some of the most incredible birds of prey.

MIGHTIEST HUNTER

Harpy eagles can pluck small monkeys out of trees and crush their skulls with powerful talons.

HEAVYWEIGHT

This title goes to the Andean condor, with some weighing in at more than 30 pounds (14 kg)—about as much as a medium-size dog. They also have the widest wingspans, up to 10 feet (3 m).

RAPTOR RAP HARPY EAGLES' TALONS ARE UP TO FIVE INCHES (13 CM) LONG—LONGER THAN A BEAR'S CLAWS!

SPEEDSTER

Peregrine falcons can dive after prey at speeds of 200 miles an hour (322 km/h).

KEENEST EYESIGHT

Eagles are believed to see up to five times better than humans, which allows them to spot a rabbit hopping through the woods half a mile (805 m) away.

BEST HEARING

While barn owls have excellent night vision, it's their sense of hearing that is tops in the animal world. A barn owl can pinpoint where a mouse is simply by listening to its footsteps on the forest floor.

A PHOTOGRAPHIC DIAGRAM

BEAK

All birds have a beak or bill specially designed for eating. The beaks of birds of prey are razor sharp and hook-shaped, which make them perfect for tearing flesh from bone.

RAPTORS UNITE,

AND SHOW YOUR SUPER BIRD

features! All birds have feathers, two feet, tails, and beaks or bills in common. Most build nests, and they all lay eggs. But that's where some of the similarities end. Raptors have specialized body parts that make them some of the world's best hunters and most skilled fliers.

EYES

Like people, birds of prey have eyes on the front of their heads, which gives them binocular vision to aid in depth perception.

TALONS

Most birds have claws for scratching the dirt or clinging on to perches. But birds of prey have knifelike talons and a viselike grip. Unlike the claws on other animals such as cats and bears, talons are muscled appendages that can grasp and snatch up prey.

WINGS

Raptors are skilled fliers, and unlike other birds, they are adept at four types of flying: gliding, flapping, soaring, and hovering. This is all thanks to their powerful wings. Most other birds can only do two or three types of flying.

TAIL

Birds of prey have flexible tails specially designed for hunting maneuvers. They can fan their tail feathers out to soar overhead as they scan the ground for prey, then fold their tail feathers together for a speedy dive. They can even twist their tail feathers to help them steer as they chase after flying prey.

OSPREY

A bald eagle flies off with its prey. Bald eagles like to live and hunt near water, including lakes, ocean coasts, rivers, and marshes.

2
RAPTOR LIFE

NEST SWEET NEST

SPRING IS THE SEASON OF LOVE FOR
MOST ANIMALS, INCLUDING BIRDS OF PREY. IT'S WHEN THEY
return to their breeding grounds, search out a mate—if they don't already have one—set up a comfy nest, and start a new family. The main reason is that spring is also the time when food is most plentiful.

A long-legged buzzard brings a lizard to feed its hungry chicks.

DUTY TO DEFEND
In most species of animals, males tend to be larger than females. Males are often the ones to establish and defend territory. This size difference is reversed for many raptors, probably because of the roles they play in reproduction and rearing. The smaller males are more agile and can be the more efficient hunters. The larger females spend more time incubating the eggs and protecting the nest. Even so, males and females generally share in the efforts, from finding food to sitting on eggs to raising young.

RAPTOR RAP FALCONS DON'T BUILD THEIR OWN NESTS. INSTEAD THEY REUSE NESTS BUILT BY OTHER BIRDS.

MI CASA ES SU CASA

Most birds of prey are solitary creatures. They hunt alone and only pair up when it's time to start a family. Some, such as black vultures and turkey vultures, are social creatures that live in communal roosts and often share meals. As the sun sets, hundreds of birds may gather and perch in neighboring trees. Roosting and flying around together makes it easier to find food. With more eyes on the ground, there is a higher chance that a tasty, rotting carcass will be found.

ONE MATE AT A TIME

Birds of prey tend to be monogamous, meaning most only have one mate at a time. They may have a different partner each breeding season, like snail kites do, or change mates every couple of years, like ospreys do. Some mate for life, such as black vultures.

These urban red-tailed hawks are nesting on the casing of an air conditioner in New York City.

BIRDIE DIGS

Unlike most other birds, New World vultures don't build traditional nests of twigs and sticks. They scrape out a hollow area in a rotting tree or in a cliff to use as a home for their young. Burrowing owls most often find an old burrow or animal den underground to use as a nest. But as their name suggests, they can also dig out their own nest.

SPRUCING UP THE OLD NEST

Most birds build new nests every year, but not birds of prey. When eagles fly back to their spring feeding grounds, they simply add a fresh coat of greenery and some new twigs to the old aerie. They will use the same nest year after year. Over time, some eagle's nests have grown to incredible size, with the largest found being almost 10 feet (3 m) wide and weighing more than 4,409 pounds (2,000 kg).

SOMETHING'S HATCHING!

LIKE ALL BIRDS, BIRDS OF PREY
START THEIR LIVES AS EGGS. MOST BIRDS OF PREY LAY
one clutch of eggs a year, but some, like the California condor, take a break from the difficulties of child rearing and only lay eggs every other year.

Getting out of an egg isn't as easy as it may seem. There's no door or secret escape hatch. But all birds, including birds of prey, have an egg tooth. This sharp knob on the bird's beak helps it cut through the shell from the inside out. The egg tooth falls off several days after the bird hatches. This chick was born at a condor captive-breeding facility.

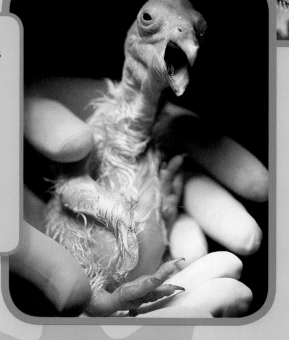

The California condor is the largest North American land bird. It can weigh up to 31 pounds (14 kg).

SMALLER BIRDS OF PREY WILL LAY AN EGG EVERY **DAY OR TWO**, WHILE **LARGER SPECIES** MAY TAKE **SEVERAL DAYS** TO LAY **EACH EGG**.

RAPTOR RAP A CALIFORNIA CONDOR EGG CAN BE MORE THAN FOUR INCHES (10 CM) LONG AND WEIGH HALF A POUND (0.23 KG).

THE THREE R's

Adult birds of prey feed their young whatever they're best at catching, from insects to other birds. But a common diet for raptors to feed their young includes the three R's:

- Rodents
- Reptiles
- Rabbits

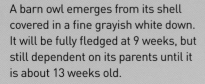

A barn owl emerges from its shell covered in a fine grayish white down. It will be fully fledged at 9 weeks, but still dependent on its parents until it is about 13 weeks old.

LIFE CYCLE OF A GOLDEN EAGLE

Not all birds of prey have the same life cycle, but they are similar. For example, barn owls average 30 days to hatching and spend 64 days as fledglings, while peregine falcon eggs take between 29 and 32 days to hatch.

0-45 DAYS

Egg: Golden eagles lay an average of two eggs in a clutch. Both males and females take turns incubating the eggs.

EGG

45-80 DAYS

Nestling: A bird is born featherless and blind, but it gains its sight and develops white, fluffy down feathers after a few days. A nestling relies on its parents for food.

NESTLING

80-120 DAYS

Fledgling: At this point in its life, the young bird is starting to outgrow the nest. So it's time to stretch its wings. It learns how to fly and also to hunt from watching its parents.

FLEDGLING

120 DAYS-5 YEARS

Juvenile: Now able to fly and feed itself, the bird is independent of its parents. It flies off to find its own territory. At this stage of life, most juvenile raptors have different coloring than adults. Juvenile golden eagles have white patches on their tails and wings that will disappear as they mature.

JUVENILE

5-30 YEARS:

Adult: A golden eagle mates for life and can live up to 30 years. And once it mates, it often returns to the same nest every breeding season.

ADULT

BIRD SENSE

THE MOST DIFFICULT

PART ABOUT BEING A PREDATOR MAY BE finding something to eat. It's not like a raptor can take a bus to the grocery store. In addition, prey animals also have a few tricks up their sleeves (or wings) to thwart predators, from camouflage that mimics their surroundings to being poisonous to eat. But birds of prey have honed their senses to help them hunt down food.

BIRD'S-EYE VIEW

Birds of prey have two eyes located on the front of their heads, which gives them binocular vision and provides them with depth perception. But unlike humans, whose eyes face forward, birds of prey eyes are angled slightly to the side. This gives them a wider range of vision and greater depth perception than humans.

When diving to snag fish out of the water or to snatch up a snake off the ground, having excellent depth perception is a must—for safety reasons. If birds of prey cannot tell the distance between themselves and their prey to the fraction of an inch, they could either end up taking a swim or going splat on the ground.

Proportionally, birds of prey have larger eyes than other animals—one reason why their eyesight is so sharp.

RAPTOR RAP OWLS HAVE THREE EYELIDS ON EACH EYE.

TURKEY VULTURE

WHAT'S THAT SMELL?

For the most part, scientists don't believe birds of prey have a very developed sense of smell. There is one exception though—turkey vultures. As they circle overhead on wind currents, they rely on smell, using their noses—those openings toward the top of their beaks—more than any other sense. Turkey vultures are carrion-eaters, so their highly developed sense of smell helps to sniff out rotting meat.

TO EAT OR NOT TO EAT

Raptors are able to detect tastes, such as sweet, salty, sour, and bitter, similar to how humans taste food. Scientists also believe that raptors' sense of taste is so discerning that it can help them avoid harmful—sometimes poisonous—foods.

SHARP-SHINNED HAWK

WHAT'S THAT YOU SAY?

While day-active birds of prey use binocular vision to pinpoint where their prey is, some owls can do that with their ears. Barn owls, for example, have large ear holes to take in more sound. But the truly unique feature is that their ears are at different heights on the sides of their heads. This gives them the ability to triangulate what they hear and pinpoint exactly from how far away and where a sound is coming. Owls have been known to snag prey in near-complete darkness, relying almost solely on their sense of hearing.

ON THE HUNT

AS IF EXTRAORDINARY
SENSES OF SIGHT AND HEARING, DEADLY
talons, and powerful beaks weren't enough, birds of prey have developed some sneaky tricks to make them deadly hunters.

A tawny owl has its head turned to look over its back.

SILENT BUT DEADLY
Owls have a unique wing design. When most birds fly, the wind rushes over the feathery surface of their wings, somewhat like an airplane's wings. This rushing wind creates a whooshing sound, which prey can hear. Owls have a comblike edge on their flight feathers. This breaks up the air rushing over their wings and muffles the whooshing sound.

OWLS SWALLOW THEIR PREY WHOLE: SKIN, BONES, AND ALL. THEN THEY COUGH UP PELLETS, WHICH ARE ANY PARTS OF A PREY ANIMAL THAT THEY COULDN'T DIGEST.

HEAD TURNERS
Sometimes keeping still is the best way to catch prey. If all is quiet, then mice and rabbits and other critters might think it's safe. Owls have tricks to help them stay silent while waiting for prey. Humans can move their eyes around in the sockets—up and down, side to side, and all around—to see in many directions without even moving our heads. Owls do not have this ability. Their eye movement is limited, but they can do something even cooler. Owls have a unique tissue and bone structure in their necks that allows them to turn their heads around 270 degrees—that's almost all the way around! This allows them to sit still on their perches, only moving their heads as they scan the forest around them.

RAPTOR RAP   PEREGRINE FALCONS EAT PIGEONS IN CITIES—DIVING AND CATCHING THEIR PREY IN MIDAIR.

An osprey grasps a freshly caught fish.

TAKING THE PLUNGE

While eagles will skim just above the surface of a lake or river as they snatch up fish, ospreys are a little more gung ho. They will hover above the water and actually plunge into it. As they go in for the kill, they will spread their wings and thrust out their talons. Sometimes they completely submerse themselves. Then they have to flap their wings vigorously to lift themselves and their catch back out of the water and to take flight again.

RABBITS BEWARE!

As if one bird of prey circling overhead isn't dangerous enough for small animals, some raptors hunt in packs! It's a trick Harris's hawks are known for. Together, a group of them will search the countryside for rabbits. When a rabbit is spotted, the hawks will surround it and swoop in for the kill. Or if need be, some of the hawks will dive in to flush the rabbit out of a brush or some shrubs while others wait to pounce when the rabbit makes a break for it.

HARRIS'S HAWK

EXPLORER'S CORNER

I have spent a good amount of time doing research in Kenya. I have been lucky enough to witness the hunting behavior of African fish eagles. The power and precision with which these eagles swoop down from their perch and snatch fish from the water is spectacular! On the other hand, I have also seen red-tailed hawks hunting small mammals such as field mice and gophers near my home in California, so you don't necessarily have to travel far to get out and develop an appreciation for birds of prey.

RED KITE

TARGET ACQUIRED

We already know that birds of prey have superior binocular vision. It's easy to see how this aids in spotting prey, but it also aids in sneaking up on unsuspecting critters. While day-active birds of prey soar hundreds of feet above the ground scanning for prey, they are also out of eyesight of the animals that they are hunting. Their prey are unaware of the danger circling above. Then they dive, swooping down so fast that by the time an animal realizes it's in danger, the raptor's deadly talons are striking.

A PHOTO GALLERY

PICK A FAVORITE!

BIRDS OF PREY

ARE SURE TO CLAW THEIR way onto your list of favorite fliers. From majestic eagles to dive-bomber peregrine falcons to elegant kestrels, they are such diverse and remarkable creatures that it's hard to pick a number one. Take a look at these beauties, appearing now in the sky near you!

The bearded vulture, or lammergeier, is a symbol of good luck in Persian mythology.

Egyptian vultures feed on carrion and the eggs of other birds. They sometimes use stones or small rocks as hammers to break open the shells of eggs they want to eat.

With its wildly colorful head, the king vulture is one of the prettiest vultures. It was described in early birding books as a "painted vulture."

You don't want to break up this fight! An adult Steller's sea-eagle lets a juvenile know whose territory it has flown into by nearly knocking it out of the sky.

Don't mess with a secretary bird. It looks like an eagle mixed with a crane, and it is known to use its long legs and clawed feet to stomp on snakes.

This bird is so hungry he could eat a monkey. No, seriously. The Philippine eagle is sometimes called the monkey eagle because one of its prey is the long-tailed macaque.

3

BIRDS OF A FEATHER

Hoo, hoo, hoo are you looking at? A group of owls is called a parliament. These parliamentarians are hanging out in a field, looking for food.

EYES ON THE SKIES

BIRDS OF PREY ARE SUPREME
HUNTING MACHINES, WITH BODIES MADE FOR PURSUING,
killing, and eating other animals. Their incredible bodies and fantastic flight skills make them awesome creatures to watch.

SNAIL KITE

ESCARGOT
Some kites have thin, hook-shaped beaks for plucking snails out of their shells.

HISSSSSS
Unlike other birds, Old World vultures don't have voice boxes, so they grunt and hiss to communicate.

GRIFFON VULTURE

HARRIER

STAYING LOW TO THE GROUND
Harriers tend to fly low to the ground, swooping up and down as they follow the contours of their surroundings.

WEAKLINGS
While eagles and other birds of prey have powerful talons, vultures are the weaklings of the bunch. They do not need to use their talons to kill prey, since they eat carrion.

RAPTOR RAP THE F-22 FIGHTER JET IS CALLED THE RAPTOR BECAUSE OF ITS SPEED.

PALE CHANTING GOSHAWK

I SWOOP FOR YOU

"Hawk" is a general term that covers a wide variety of birds, mostly raptors that live in wooded areas and swoop down from perches to snatch up prey. They have short wings and long tails to help with their maneuverability through trees.

EASTERN SCREECH-OWL

COMING IN LOUD AND CLEAR

Owls have facial discs, making it look like they have two satellite dishes around their eyes. Well, these features actually work like satellite dishes and aid in hearing by helping direct sound waves to their ears.

They perch, they swoop, they soar, and they may even live right near you! Birds of prey are amazing to watch but even experienced bird-watchers can have difficulty identifying them in the sky. Bird-watchers carefully examine the heads, wings, tails, legs, size, and flight patterns of birds. Then they compare what they see with the bird's known coloring and markings. Sometimes you can identify a bird by its silhouette. Look up—way up—and here's what you might find.

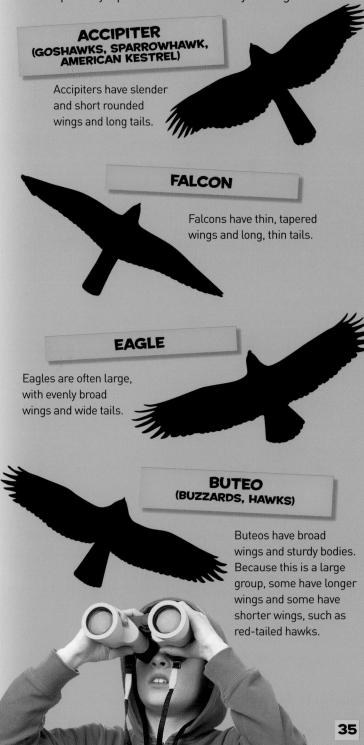

ACCIPITER
(GOSHAWKS, SPARROWHAWK, AMERICAN KESTREL)

Accipiters have slender and short rounded wings and long tails.

FALCON

Falcons have thin, tapered wings and long, thin tails.

EAGLE

Eagles are often large, with evenly broad wings and wide tails.

BUTEO
(BUZZARDS, HAWKS)

Buteos have broad wings and sturdy bodies. Because this is a large group, some have longer wings and some have shorter wings, such as red-tailed hawks.

A BIRD IN THE HAND

THROUGHOUT HISTORY, PEOPLE HAVE USED VARIOUS TOOLS TO HUNT: WOODEN STICKS, STONE AXES, BOW AND ARROWS, AND YES . . .

birds of prey. While people today look at falconry as a sport, hundreds and even thousands of years ago, people used trained raptors to hunt for them. After all, a bird of prey is much more deadly and efficient at killing small animals than a spear or an arrow.

MONGOLIAN EAGLE HUNTERS

Many experts believe that falconry originated in the open plains of Mongolia nearly 6,000 to 8,000 years ago. Using golden eagles to hunt for foxes and hares is a tradition among the Kazakh people that is still practiced today. Eagle hunters train their birds with a hood until the hunter and eagle become a team. Hunters are also skilled horse riders, who ride with their eagle perched on one of their arms.

A hunter holds his eagle at the Altai Kazakh Eagle Festival in the mountains of Mongolia. Every year, eagle hunters gather there to compete in a hunt for foxes and hares.

RAPTOR RAP THE AZTEC OF CENTRAL AMERICA PRACTICED FALCONRY.

The medieval saying "a bird in the hand is worth two in the bush" refers to how one trained falcon was more valuable than two wild falcons. It means "don't be greedy" and "stick with what you have rather than chase something you might never get."

BIRD OF KINGS

During the Middle Ages, falconry become popular in Europe. Medieval nobles hunted with birds of prey for sport and as a way to show off. A person's status in society determined what kind of bird of prey they used. The more important a person was, the bigger or faster their bird was. A king might hunt with a gyrfalcon, the largest of the falcons, while a knight would hunt with a smaller saker falcon.

MODERN FALCONERS

Today, falconry isn't just a hunting sport, it's also a way to protect precious fruit and vineyard crops from being eaten by other birds. Some farmers hire falconers to scare away birds that eat their crops. But it's not easy to take part in falconry. Across Europe and North America, many birds of prey are protected—in some countries it's illegal to own them, while in others you have to meet certain requirements to be allowed to own one. Still, it is estimated that 10,000 people in North America alone practice falconry.

Falconry uses special equipment. Here are some of the important pieces:

ANKLETS
Leather anklets attached to a leash keep the bird tethered down.

HOOD
The hood helps keep the bird calm and focused.

LEASH
A leash is used to keep the bird of prey on a perch or gloved hand.

THICK LEATHER GLOVE
This is probably the most important piece of equipment, as all birds of prey have razor-sharp talons.

RAPTORS AND ROBINS

BIRDS OF PREY SHARE MANY
THINGS IN COMMON WITH OTHER BIRDS, FROM having feathers to laying eggs. They have two feet and a beak. But that's not all. Many birds, from robins to eagles, have territories where they feed and breed. Songbirds and raptors also both migrate.

SING ME A SONG
People expect backyard birds to sing, chirp, and twitter. That's why they set out bird feeders to attract them. But birds of prey are also very vocal. Owls may hoot, and hawks may screech, but some raptors sing in their own somewhat loud and screechy way like the merlin's *ki-ki-kee* and the American kestrel's *klee-klee-klee*.

Birds of prey will also screech to tell other raptors to get out of their territory. They sometimes call out to tell their mates and young to tell them where they are.

COLOR ME BROWN
Male and female songbirds have different coloring, with males being more brightly colored than females. But male and female birds of prey tend to be similar in coloring. That doesn't mean there aren't noticeable color differences within a raptor species. A typical red-tailed hawk will have a light red-brown underwing and belly feathers, with light red-tan tail feathers. But they also have other color variations, or morphs.

WESTERN RED-TAILED HAWK

A red-tailed hawk's belly and covert feathers have dark spots, with distinct lines on the tail.

DARK MORPH

In a dark morph of a red-tailed hawk, the belly is dark brown with patches of white, and the covert feathers are also dark brown.

LIGHT MORPH

A light morph has few markings on the underwings and belly, as they appear almost white.

RAPTOR RAP FERRUGINOUS HAWKS HAVE BEEN KNOWN TO SCARE COYOTES AWAY FROM THE BIRDS' NESTS.

It's an eagle party! A group of bald eagles, called a convocation, sit on rocks. They migrate and gather in some areas of North America each winter to feast on spawning salmon.

IT'S ALL ABOUT THE FOOD

Animals migrate, or change locations from season to season, because of food. Often this occurs in spring and fall. Migration is not unique to birds. But bird migrations seem the most dramatic, as thousands of birds sometimes migrate together in flocks. Birds of prey migrate if food gets scarce, moving to a warmer climate where food is more plentiful. The distances raptors migrate varies greatly. Ospreys may fly thousands of miles, from Canada to Argentina, while bald eagles fly a few hundred miles, from Canada to the United States.

Two greater spotted eagles battle for territory.

KESTREL

THAT'S MY TERRITORY

Birds have territories, or areas in which they live, breed, and search for food. While a songbird's territory (thanks to a bird feeder) may only be the size of your backyard, birds of prey will range over many square miles in their hunt for prey. This is mainly because prey animals—their food—are more scarce and difficult to find than seeds and insects. A hawk may have to scour its territory for hours before spotting a rabbit or lizard to swoop down on. Birds of prey will use their deadly weapons—beaks and talons—to defend their territory from other raptors.

RAPTOR REPORT

WHILE THERE ARE HUNDREDS
OF TYPES OF BIRDS OF PREY, AND MANY

millions of raptors, not all species have healthy populations. Several birds of prey are in danger of becoming extinct. Ornithologists (bird scientists) play an important role in bird conservation. They can often determine what is threatening a raptor population through studying the habits of birds of prey, from their diet to migratory patterns. Sitting atop the food chain, birds of prey and all predators are an important part of a healthy environment. A kite may eat hundreds of insects a day. Knowing how many kites live in an area also shows how many grasshoppers and moths live there, and that in turn helps determine what the plant life is like. A healthy population of predators is a sign of a healthy environment.

To study birds, researchers attach bands, collars, and radio transmitters to them.

EXPLORER'S CORNER

Some of my current research focuses on understanding how humans have changed bird communities in the Channel Islands off southern California, where I live. For hundreds of years, bald eagles lived and nested on these islands. However, human influences—chemical pesticide pollution, poaching, and invasive species—made bald eagles disappear from the islands by the mid-1900s. However, a team of scientists began a bald eagle reintroduction project on the islands in the 1980s, and now, after decades of work, bald eagles live and nest on the islands. Work like this keeps me motivated to learn more about Earth's ecosystems and create more success stories.

PELLET COUNT, ANYONE?

Picking apart a raptor's pellet—undigested remains from its last meal—may not sound pleasant, but it's a good way to study the food chain. Scientists can tell what an owl has been eating by what's in the pellets it regurgitates and then learn what other animal species are thriving in an area. They can also estimate an owl population by the number of pellets they collect.

OWL PELLET

RAPTOR RAP LEAD POISONING IS THE LEADING CAUSE OF CALIFORNIA CONDOR DEATHS.

FIXING BROKEN WINGS

It can be a dangerous world out there, even for a mighty bird of prey. Eagles get hit by cars as they're eating roadkill. Hawks fly into power lines. Pollutants, from lead waste to oil spills, can sicken raptors. Luckily, there are bird hospitals and rehab centers to help injured and sick birds. They have trained vets who specialize in working with large birds. They help fix broken wings and legs and then release their patients back into the wild. A center such as the Raptor Center at the University of Minnesota can treat more than 700 sick and injured raptors a year. They also educate people about birds of prey.

HATCH AND RELEASE

Captive-breeding programs are a way of increasing the population of birds, especially those that are threatened or endangered in the wild. Breeding programs bring the birds together in a safe environment where they are paired with a mate to breed and raise chicks. The goal of most breeding programs is to eventually reintroduce the captive-bred birds into the wild, such as was done with the California condor.

BACK FROM THE BRINK

One of the most amazing stories of an endangered animal coming back from the brink of extinction is the California condor. These New World vultures are found only in remote areas of California and Arizona. But still, people have encroached on their territory, and human impact, from habitat destruction to stealing the rare eggs—laid one every other year—has been brutal. Eventually, the population of California condors dropped to just a handful of birds. So scientists began to collect eggs for controlled incubation and captured the remaining 22 birds that were in the wild. California condors have since been reintroduced into the wild, with more than 400 birds now known to exist.

CALIFORNIA CONDOR

Talk to the hand! A puppet is used to rear a California condor chick in a captive-breeding program. The puppet prevents the chick from believing humans are its parents.

RAPTOR COMPARISONS

YOU vs. A BIRD OF PREY

THROUGHOUT THIS BOOK YOU HAVE READ MANY impressive facts about birds of prey, from their superhuman senses to their amazing abilities to hunt down prey. Now check out how you stack up against these mighty predators.

EAGLE EYES

The average person has 20/20 vision. That means at 20 feet (6.1 m) away, you can clearly see letters that are about one-third of an inch (0.8 cm) tall. But eagles can have 20/4 vision, meaning that they see at 20 feet (6.1 m) what the average person sees at four feet (1.2 m). Or to make that sound more impressive, what you see clearly at 20 feet (6.1 m), they may see at 100 feet (30 m)—that's five times better than the average person.

BUG-EATING CONTEST

Smaller birds tend to be more active and use more energy, so in turn, they need more food. A small kite might eat up to 20 percent of its body weight in insects a day. That would be like saying if you weighed 100 pounds (45 kg), you would have to eat 20 pounds (9 kg) of moths and grasshoppers, or 40 half-pound (.23 kg) hamburgers.

WINGSPAN

You may stand taller than a 4-foot (1.2-m) Andean condor, but it would take you and a friend spreading your arms as wide as you can to match its 10-foot (3-m) wingspan.

DIVING SPEED

When a roller coaster drops out from under you, you scream as you speed down the track at what feels like a death-defying speed. The Formula Rossa in Abu Dhabi is considered the world's fastest roller coaster. Riders plunge from its 174-foot (53-m) drop at speeds of up to 150 miles an hour (241 km/h), but even that incredible speed doesn't match a peregrine falcon's 200 mile-an-hour-plus (322-km/h) dive when it chases after prey.

GET YOUR RUNNING SHOES ON

At your top speed, you can probably run around 15 miles an hour (24 km/h) for a short burst. A golden eagle can fly five times as fast, or around 75 miles an hour (121 km/h).

FUN WITH BIRDS OF PREY

A snowy owl sits in the snow looking for mice or lemmings to catch and eat.

FLY LIKE AN EAGLE

RED-TAILED HAWK

BIRDS OF PREY ARE SOME
OF THE MOST SKILLED FLIERS. THEY CAN
soar for hours and gracefully glide to the ground. They can flap their wings in powerful strokes to launch themselves skyward, or tuck their wings close to their body as they dive after prey.

RAPTOR RAP   RED-TAILED HAWKS ARE THE MOST COMMON HAWKS IN NORTH AMERICA.

KING VULTURE

GREAT HORNED OWL

TEST YOUR SKILLS:

Match the skill with the bird of prey.

A

GREAT HORNED OWL

B

PEREGRINE FALCON

C

RED-TAILED HAWK

D

WHITE-TAILED KITE

E

KING VULTURE

1. HIGH DIVE

When these birds target prey below them, they tuck their wings and straighten their tail feathers to narrow their bodies into feathery bullets.

2. SOARING

Once they are in the sky, these birds can soar for hours without having to flap their wings. They have strong, wide wings perfect for catching air currents, so they ride thermals, or columns of hot rising air, to stay aloft.

3. HOVERING

These birds face into the wind and flap their wings to remain stable in the air. This skill makes it look like they are hanging over a clump of grass or bush, watching and waiting for their rodent prey.

4. FLAPPING

With their long wingspan, these raptors only need a few powerful and strong beats to lift them into the air.

5. GLIDING

As they hunt, these birds drop from their perches and swoop down on their prey without even flapping their wings.

A LITTLE BIRD TOLD ME

THERE ARE A LOT OF
BIRDBRAINED STORIES ABOUT
birds of prey. Are you the rare bird who can tell fact from fiction with these tales?

Ⓐ THE TERM "HOODWINK," MEANING TO FOOL SOMEONE, ORIGINATED WITH THE ANCIENT PRACTICE OF FALCONRY.

Ⓑ BIRDS OF PREY HAVE CARRIED OFF CHILDREN.

Ⓒ SOME BIRDS OF PREY USE VOMIT AND URINE AS A PROTECTIVE MECHANISM.

Ⓓ OWLS ONLY HUNT AT NIGHT.

A. FACT Falconry is a way of hunting that uses trained birds of prey to find and catch small mammals, such as rabbits. Falcons are keen-sighted birds that are aware of their surroundings, but falconers need calm birds that are not distracted by their environment. They use leather hoods to cover their falcon's head and eyes. The practice of hooding a falcon was called hoodwinking because it kept the bird "in the dark" before sending it out to catch prey. The term eventually was used to describe fooling or tricking someone.

RAPTOR RAP COOPER'S HAWKS ARE SOMETIMES CALLED CHICKEN HAWKS BECAUSE THEY EAT CHICKENS.

B. FICTION

While there are many fanciful stories about this happening, none have been documented. They are simply myths. The largest birds of prey only weigh upwards of 30 pounds (14 kg).The average weight of a one-year-old child is more than 20 pounds (9 kg), much too heavy for even the mighty harpy falcon, which hunts small monkeys, to carry off.

C. FACT

If frightened, black vultures will vomit to lighten their load for a quick getaway from predators. They will also urinate on themselves to stay cool, clean, and disease-free. The urine acts like sweat to cool their bodies off, and the acid in the urine destroys bacteria and organisms that cause disease.

D. FICTION

While most owls are nocturnal, or night hunters, some hunt during twilight hours at dawn and dusk, and a few species, such as the burrowing owl, snowy owl, and the short-eared owl, are day hunters. Because of their shape, owls' eyes let in more light, aiding their night vision.

WHAT'S YOUR BIRD OF PREY-SONALITY?

THEY ARE THE TOP OF THE AVIAN FOOD CHAIN

AND MASTERS OF THE SKIES, BUT EACH BIRD OF PREY HAS ITS PREFERRED habitat, prey of choice, and favorite nesting place. Ever wonder what kind of raptor you might be? Take this quiz to find out!

1 What foods would you prefer to nosh on?

A. Tasty fish, the fresher the better
B. Roadside dining and fresh snacks
C. Late-night snacks are the best
D. Anything that comes already prepared

2 What's your crib like, birdie?

A. Ahoy! Near the sea or other body of water
B. Nothing is better than the freedom of the open prairie.
C. On a farm with a big red barn to perch on
D. In a high-up tree house or tall tower

3 Your family life could best be described as:

A. Just me and my best bud!
B. Quiet and cozy with my parents and me
C. A big family. We stay close, even though I don't like to share with them.
D. All my friends are my family and come over for dinner anytime.

4 Your "fly" style includes:

A. A white hat and scarf
B. A red hat and leggings
C. A light gray-brown jacket
D. Black. Nothing but black

5 People say you are:

A. Serious to the core
B. The class clown
C. A homebody
D. Sociable—where's the party?

WHAT DOES YOUR PREY-SONALITY SAY ABOUT YOU?

IF YOU SCORED MOSTLY

A's: You share traits with the majestic bald eagle. A water lover, you prefer the company of a long-term companion, and you perch above all the rest.

IF YOU SCORED MOSTLY

B's: You're similar to the bateleur eagle. You're a frequent flier and sub-Saharan sun lover. Known for your flashy style, your funny walk has given you the nickname "tightrope walker."

IF YOU SCORED MOSTLY

C's: You're quite the hoot (or rather, screech) like your bird counterpart, the barn owl. You like to stick close to home and hang out with a few neighborhood pals.

IF YOU SCORED MOSTLY

D's: You're like the friend-loving turkey vulture. A native of North America, you're not too fussy about what you eat, as long as it's smelly and easy to come by.

BALD EAGLE

TURKEY VULTURE

BATELEUR EAGLE

BARN OWL

RAPTOR RAP VULTURES SOMETIMES FLY AS HIGH AS 10,000 FEET (3,048 M) ABOVE THE GROUND.

BIRDS OF PREY IN CULTURE

USA 39

Hawkman

2006

DEADLY HUNTERS WITH REMARKABLE

SKILL, BIRDS OF PREY HAVE BEEN REVERED AND WORSHIPPED for thousands of years. Often viewed as symbols of power and fearlessness, birds of prey are depicted on money, in movies, and in myths and legends.

WISE AS AN OWL

The idea of owls being wise animals dates back to ancient Greece. The owl was a symbol of Athena, the goddess of wisdom. But in reality, there's really no proof that owls are smarter than other birds of prey. Hawks are actually believed to be the smartest raptors.

The superhero Hawkman first appeared in comics in 1940 and was on a U.S. stamp in 2006. The comic hero Hawkeye has appeared in several Avengers movies. He was first a villain and then became a "straight shooter."

HAWKEYED SUPERHEROES

Several comic book superheroes have bird of prey traits. There's even a DC Comics series and superhero team called Birds of Prey. Those superheroes and superheroines—including the Hawk, Hawkgirl, and Nightwing—fight bad guys in Gotham City and Metropolis. Hawkman is also a DC Comics superhero who is a member of the Justice League of America. His superpowers include hawklike sight and the ability to fly. In the Marvel Comics series Hawkeye, the superhero is a master archer who works alongside the Avengers.

RAPTOR RAP IN SOME CULTURES, AN OWL'S HOOT IS A SIGN THAT BAD WEATHER IS APPROACHING.

LORD OF THE BIRDS

Because they both ruled the sky, birds of prey were often connected with the sky gods by ancient people. In Egyptian myths, Horus was not only the ruler of the gods, but he was also the falcon god. He was depicted as either a giant bird of prey or a man with a falcon head.

SACRED FEATHERS

In many native North American cultures, eagles are considered sacred animals. They appear as both messengers to the Creator of the world and as the Creator's favorite creatures. Because of this, eagle feathers are highly prized. They are given as gifts of honor and used in ceremonies and as part of ceremonial dress. In some areas, it is against the law for non-native North Americans to sell or trade wild eagle feathers.

THE EAGLE HAS LANDED

The famous words "the *Eagle* has landed" were spoken by NASA astronaut Neil Armstrong in 1969 when the lunar module (space capsule) carrying him and fellow astronaut Buzz Aldrin landed on the moon. The module was named the *Eagle,* but it wasn't the first or last vessel to use the name.

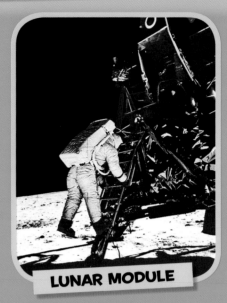

LUNAR MODULE

From representing the bravest Aztec soldiers, the eagle warriors, to French emperor Napoleon's Imperial Eagle, eagles have also been an important military symbol. This is probably because of the eagle's regal posture and deadly strikes when swooping down on prey. The double-headed eagle was a symbol of several historic armies and empires, including the Holy Roman Empire.

RUSSIAN EMPIRE MILITARY EAGLE

Eagles have been the mascots for many sports teams, including professional soccer, football, and hockey teams. The name Eagle has also been used for clothing stores and for a famous infantry division of the U.S. Army—the 101st Airborne Division "Screaming Eagles."

MANCHESTER CITY FOOTBALL CLUB

BEHIND THE SHOT WITH HILLARY S. YOUNG

Although not birds of prey, tufted puffins also live on Hawadax Island today. Their presence, along with gulls, sandpipers, and petrels, is a sign that the island is again becoming a refuge for birds.

HAWADAX ISLAND IS A SMALL
ISLAND FAR OFF MAINLAND ALASKA. IN 1780, WHEN A

Japanese ship crashed on the shores of Hawadax, the island was overrun with birds—seabirds nesting on the cliffs, sparrows calling in the grasslands, and eagles and falcons happily feasting on the abundant food. However, that ship changed everything—it had rats on its decks. When the ship sank, the rats swam to shore and made a home on Hawadax.

The rats ate the eggs and chicks of all the seabirds and land birds, and these birds rapidly began to disappear—leaving no food for the birds of prey except for rats themselves. The rats were so numerous that the island was officially renamed Rat Island. By 2008, the island was nearly silent, with hardly a bird to be seen. Land managers and researchers decided to do something about it, so they removed ALL the rats. Every last one.

I arrived on this beautiful, cold island in 2010, two years after the rats had been removed. I was part of a team whose job it was to see if the island was recovering, and to see what was happening to the birds of prey after the rat removal. What we witnessed was the beginning of a remarkable islandwide recovery. Bird species that had long been gone from the island were back and numbers were up.

But the high point of the trip was when the team found a peregrine falcon nest on the top of a craggy peak at the end of a long day's hike! Peregrine falcons are amazing creatures—they have sharp pointed beaks and make deep diving flights. In fact, their diving speeds make them the fastest animal on Earth as they reach stoop, or downward swoop, speeds of more than 200 miles an hour (322 km/h). They are so fast that they primarily hunt in the air—and thus mainly eat other birds. So their presence was a wonderful sign of the successful recovery of the island population.

Today, the island has been renamed Hawadax once again, and it has become a model of conservation success. Many bird species, including peregrine falcons and bald eagles, now breed and are flourishing on the island's rocky shores. Looking at this picture reminds me of how much good we can do for birds when we put our minds to it.

RUSSIA

Alaska CANADA

HAWADAX ISLAND U.S.

Pacific Ocean

Not a rat's nest to be found! Hillary S. Young took this photo of a peregrine nest while doing research on Hawadax Island, Alaska.

AFTERWORD

TOP PREDATOR, TOP ECOLOGIST

WHEN WE SPY A HAWK SWOOPING DOWN FROM ABOVE, WE WANT TO STOP AND WATCH IT.

If we are lucky enough to see a bald eagle nest in the wild, we think of it as a treasure. Even dark columns of turkey vultures circling above their next carrion meal are a spellbinding sight. For thousands of years, humans have been fascinated by birds of prey, but raptors are more than just amazing deadly predators. Birds of prey help keep nature in balance. They control pest and rodent populations near farmlands. And they clean the environment of dead and diseased animals (by eating them).

Biologists call birds of prey "indicator species." It means that they are animals that help scientists observe and check the health of the environment. A bird of prey that lives in a habitat and is healthy is seen as a sign that the entire habitat is healthy. In other words, if birds of prey are thriving, good soil and water have produced healthy plant life. These plants are the food that prey animals eat. And when there is healthy prey, birds of prey have plenty to eat.

Birds of prey are sensitive to changes in the environment made by humans. They ingest poisons, pesticides, and toxins through their prey. Unnatural deaths are a telltale sign that the levels of pollutants are dangerously high. And while birds of prey adapt to human encroachment on their habitat, they are also harmed by the dangers of living near people. Every year, thousands of birds of prey are hit by vehicles, collide with power lines, and die through habitat loss, poisoning, and poaching.

Conservation efforts help identify and monitor threats to birds of prey populations. But don't think conservation is just for the birds. It is also an important part of protecting our own lives and the world we call home. Birds of prey help us know the health of our environment, which is important to all life on Earth. They do more for us than we do for them.

HELPING RAPTORS

It's a good thing we are so enraptured by raptors. They delight and excite and make us want to help them live and thrive. There are many organizations that have made it their mission to conserve and protect raptors and raptor habitats. Often, these organizations use donations of money or volunteers to help them accomplish their goals. Some, such as the Hawk Migration Association of North America, have monitoring sites where volunteers watch the skies during migration and keep count of birds. Others are dedicated to healing injured birds or to studying their habits or habitats.

White-tailed sea-eagles compete for territory.

You can't escape their gaze! Black kites have yellow claws and yellow eyes.

AN INTERACTIVE GLOSSARY

BIRD WORDS

What are you looking at? Owl fledglings begin to leave the nest at about 10 to 14 weeks.

YOU ARE ON YOUR WAY TO BECOMING AN

ORNITHOLOGIST. BUT BEFORE YOU START BIRD-WATCHING, READ THROUGH

this list of words and phrases to test if you are "as wise as an owl." Afterward, check out the words in action on the pages listed. Some questions have more than one answer.

1. Aerie
A large nest built by a bird of prey
[PAGE 23]

Which bird(s) of prey is known for building a large nest?

a. Andean vulture

b. bald eagle

c. burrowing owl

d. gyrfalcon

2. Camouflage
Protective coloring that helps animals blend into their surroundings
[PAGE 26]

Which are types of camouflage used by birds of prey?

a. light-colored underwing feathers

b. brightly colored feathers

c. ruffled leg feathers

d. brown and white feathery patches

3. Carrion
A dead, rotting animal
[PAGES 11, 12, 27, 30, 34, 56]

Which bird(s) of prey is known for eating carrion?

a. peregrine falcon

b. snowy owl

c. bald eagle

d. king vulture

4. Depth Perception
The ability to judge distance
[PAGES 18, 26]

What trait(s) aids in depth perception?

a. eye color

b. eyes on the side the head

c. eyes on the front of head

d. eye shape

5. Diurnal
Being active during the day
[PAGES 12, 13]

Which bird(s) of prey is diurnal?

a. harpy eagle

b. barn owl

c. turkey vulture

d. snail kite

6. Endangered
An animal at risk of extinction
[PAGE 41]

What might cause an animal to become endangered?

a. pollution

b. overhunting

c. loss of habitat

d. all of the above

7. Mate
To pair up for breeding purposes
[PAGES 22, 23, 25, 38, 41]

Which bird(s) of prey is known for mating for life?

a. osprey

b. golden eagle

c. black vulture

d. snail kite

8. Migrate
To move from one area to another
[PAGES 13, 38, 39]

Which is the main cause of animal migration?

a. changes in the weather

b. overpopulation

c. boredom

d. food scarcity

9. Nocturnal
Being active at night
[PAGES 13, 49]

Which bird(s) of prey are nocturnal?

a. harpy eagle

b. barn owl

c. turkey vulture

d. snail kite

10. Pellet
A mass of undigested bones and feathers vomited up by a bird of prey
[PAGES 28, 40]

What can an ornithologist learn from examining birds of prey's pellets?

a. health of the birds

b. what the birds eat

c. bird population

d. all of the above

11. Predator
An animal that hunts other animals for food
[PAGES 26, 40, 42, 49, 56]

Aside from birds of prey, which other animal(s) is a predator?

a. worm

b. skunk

c. alligator

d. moth

12. Talon
A sharp claw on the toe of a bird of prey
[PAGES 7, 10, 11, 12, 16, 19, 29, 34, 39]

A bird of prey's talons have an ability similar to which other animal feature?

a. a dog's paws

b. a bear's claws

c. a cat's claws

d. a human's fingers

ANSWERS: 1. b; 2. a and d; 3. c and d; 4. c; 5. a, c, and d; 6. d; 7. b and c; 8. d; 9. b; 10. d; 11. b and c; 12. d

FIND OUT MORE

Want to learn more about birds of prey? Get your claws on these resources.

WEBSITES AND PLACES TO MEET BIRDS OF PREY

Kids: Ask your parents for permission to search online.

Audubon Center for Birds of Prey
1101 Audubon Way, Maitland, FL 32751
fl.audubon.org/audubon-center-birds-prey

The Center for Birds of Prey
4872 Seewee Rd., Awendaw, SC 29429
thecenterforbirdsofprey.org

International Association for Falconry and Conservation of Birds of Prey
iaf.org

International Centre of Birds of Prey
Boulsdon House, Newent, Gloucestershire UK GL18 1JJ
icbp.org

National Geographic—Birds
video.nationalgeographic.com/video/animals/birds

Raptor Research Foundation
raptorresearchfoundation.org

World Center for Birds of Prey
5668 West Flying Hawk Ln., Boise, ID 83709
peregrinefund.org/world-center

BIRD CAMERAS TO WATCH

explore.org
explore.org/live-cams/player/live-osprey-cam

The National Geographic Society
video.nationalgeographic.com/video/dc-eaglecam-highlights

The Royal Society for the Protection of Birds
rspb.org.uk/webcams/birdsofprey

READ IT!

Birds of Prey (My First Pocket Guide)
by Amy Donovan and Michael Shafran
Washington, DC: National Geographic Society, 2003

How Fast Can a Falcon Dive? Fascinating Answers to Questions About Birds of Prey
by Peter Capainolo and Carol A. Butler
New Brunswick, NJ: Rutgers University Press, 2010

Raptor! A Kid's Guide to Birds of Prey
by Christyna M. & René Laubach and Charles W. G. Smith
North Adams, MA: Storey Books, 2002

A

Aeries 23, 61
Altai Kazakh Eagle
   Festival 36
Armstrong, Neil 53
Aves 12
Aztec 36, 53

B

Beaks **5,** 11, 12, 18, 24,
   27, 28, 34, 38
Bird-watchers 35
Breeding 22–23, 24, 25,
   38, 39, 41, 54
Buteos, 35
Buzzards 11, 12, **22,** 35

C

Camouflage 26, 61
Carnivores 10
Carrion 11, 12, 27, 30, 34,
   56, 61
Claws 11, 13, 16, 19, 30,
   31, **58,** 61
Coloring **5,** 15, 25, **30,** 35,
   38, 61
Common kestrel 15, 39,
   39
Condors 16, 24, 40, 43,
   43
Conservation 40–41, 56

D

Deaths 40, 41, 56
Dinosaurs **10,** 10
Diurnal birds 12, 61
Diving 11, 17, 19, 26, 28,
   29, 30, 43, 46, 54

E

Eagle 53
Eagles 7, 11, 12, 14–15,
   16, 17, **17,** 23, 29, 35,
   36, 38, 42, 53, 54, 61
   African fish eagles
      15, 15, 29
   Bald eagles 8, 8,
      20–21, 21, 39, 39,
      40, 50, 51, 54, 56, 61
   Bateleur eagles 50, **51,**
      51

Golden eagles **15,** 15,
   25, 25, 36, **43,** 43, 61
Greater spotted
   eagles, **39,** 39
Harpy eagles **14,** 14,
   16, 16, 61
Philippine eagles **15,**
   15, **30,** 30
Steller's sea-eagles
   6–7, 6–7, **31,** 31
White-tailed sea-
   eagles **57**
Egg teeth **25,** 25
Eggs 10, 18, 24–25, **25,**
   30, 38, 41, 54
Endangered species 41,
   61
Environment 40, 48, 56
European kestrel *see*
   common kestrel
Eyes 13, **18,** 18, 23, **26,**
   26, 28, 35, **42,** 42, 48,
   58, **58–59,** 61

F

Facial discs 13, **35,** 35
Falconry **36–37,** 36–37,
   48, 48
Falcons 7, **12,** 12, **22,** 22,
   35, 48, 53, 54,
   Gyrfalcon **15,** 15, 37,
      61
   Peregrine falcon **17,**
      17, 25, 28, 30, **43,**
      43, **47,** 47, 61
   Philippine falconet 14
   Saker falcon 37
Families 11, 12, 23, 50
   Accipitridae 12
   Cathartidae 12
   Falconidae 12
   Pandionidae 12
   Sagittariidae 12
   Strigidae 13
   Tytonidae 13
Feathers 11, 13, 14, 18,
   25, 28, 38, 47, **53,**
   53, 61
Feet 10, 12, 18, 31, 38
Flapping 12, 19, 29, 47

G

Gliding 10, 18, 46, 47

H

Habitats 14–15, 41, 50,
   56, 61
Harriers 12, 34, 34
Hatching 24–25, 25, 41
Hawadax Island 54–55,
   54–55
Hawk Migration
   Association of
   North America 57
Hawks 7, 11, 12, 41, 56
   Cooper's hawks 48
   Ferruginous hawks 38
   Goshawks 35
   Harris's hawks **29,** 29
   Red-tailed hawks **23,**
      23, 46, 46
   Sharp-shinned hawks
      27
   Sparrowhawks 35
Heads 5, 12, 14, 18, **28,**
   28, 30, 35, 48, 61
Horus **53,** 53
Hovering 19, 29, 47
Hunting 10, 12, 13, 14,
   15, 18, 19, 21, 23, 25,
   26, 28–29, 34, 36–37,
   39, 42, 46, 47, 48, 49,
   54, 61

I

Insects 7, 11, 12, 25, 39,
   40, 42

K

Kazakh people **36,** 36
Kites 12, 23, **29,** 29, **34,**
   34, 40, **42,** 42, **58,**
   58–59, 61

L

Legs 12, 35, 40, 61

M

Markings 35, 38
Migration 13, 39, 61
Mongolia 36
Monkey eagles *see*
   Philippine eagles
Monogamy 23
Myths 48–49, 52, 53

N

Nests 14, 18, **22–23,**
   22–23, 38, 40, 50, 54,
   55, 55, 56, 61
Nocturnal birds 13, 49,
   61
Northern crested
   caracara **14,** 14

O

Orders 12, 13
Ornithologists 12, 15,
   40, 61
Ospreys 7, **12,** 12, 18–19,
   23, **29,** 29, 39, 61
Owls 7, 13, 23, 27, **28,** 28,
   32–33, 32–33, 35, 38,
   40, 48, **49,** 49, 52, **60,**
   60, 61
   Barn owls **13, 17,** 17,
      25, 50, **51**
   Great horned owls, **47**
   Oriental bay owls 13
   Screech-owls **13, 35**
   Snowy owls **44–45,**
      44–45

P

Pellets 28, **40,** 40, 61
Pesticides 40, 56
Poaching 40, 56
Pollutants 40, 41, 56, 61

R

Rabbits 16, 25, 29, 39, 48
Radio transmitters **40,**
   40
Rat Island *see* Hawadax
   Island
Rehab centers 41
Rodents 7, 15, 25, 28, 45,
   47, 54, 55, 56
Roosting 23

S

Secretary birds **12,** 12,
   31, 31

Senses 11, 12, 16–17,
   18, 26, 27, 28, 29, 35,
   42, 49
Singing 38
Size 10, 14, 15, 16, 22, 24,
   35, 37, 42, 49
Snakes 26, 31
Soaring 7, 19, 29, 35, 47
Species 11
Speed 12, 17, 19, 34, 43,
   54
Superheroes **52,** 52

T

Tails 18, **19,** 19, 25, 35, 38
Talons 7, 11, 12, 16, **19,**
   19, 28, 34, 37, 39, 61
Territories 22, 25, 31, 39,
   41, 57
Tufted puffins 54

U

U.S. Army 53

V

Vultures 11, 24, 41, 61
   Black vultures, **23,** 23,
      49, 49, 61
   Griffon vultures **8–9,**
      8–9, **24,** 24
   King vultures **4–5,** 4–5,
      12, 12, 14, **30,** 30,
      47
   Turkey vultures, **27,** 27,
      50, **51,** 56, 61
Weight 16, 24, 42, 49
Wings 7, 10, 12, 16, **19,**
   19, 25, 26, 28, 38,
   43, 43, 47, 61

Y

Young, Hillary S. **7,** 7,
   54–55

Staff for This Book
Shelby Alinsky, *Project Editor*
James Hiscott, Jr., *Art Director*
Lori Epstein, *Senior Photo Editor*
Paige Towler, *Editorial Assistant*
Erica Holsclaw, *Special Projects Assistant*
Sanjida Rashid, *Design Production Assistant*
Michael Cassady, *Photo Assistant*
Carl Mehler, *Director of Maps*
Grace Hill, *Associate Managing Editor*
Mike O'Connor, *Production Editor*
Lewis R. Bassford, *Production Manager*
Rachel Faulise, *Manager, Production Services*
Susan Borke, *Legal and Business Affairs*
Neal Edwards, *Imaging*

Published by the National Geographic Society
Gary E. Knell, *President and CEO*
John M. Fahey, *Chairman of the Board*
Melina Gerosa Bellows, *Chief Education Officer*
Declan Moore, *Chief Media Officer*
Hector Sierra, *Senior Vice President and General Manager, Book Division*

Senior Management Team, Kids Publishing and Media
Nancy Laties Feresten, *Senior Vice President;* Jennifer Emmett, *Vice President, Editorial Director, Kids Books;* Julie Vosburgh Agnone, *Vice President, Editorial Operations;* Rachel Buchholz, *Editor and Vice President,* NG Kids *magazine;* Michelle Sullivan, *Vice President, Kids Digital;* Eva Absher-Schantz, *Design Director;* Jay Sumner, *Photo Director;* Hannah August, *Marketing Director;* R. Gary Colbert, *Production Director*

Digital
Anne McCormack, *Director;* Laura Goertzel, Sara Zeglin, *Producers;* Jed Winer, *Special Projects Assistant;* Emma Rigney, *Creative Producer;* Brian Ford, *Video Producer;* Bianca Bowman, *Assistant Producer;* Natalie Jones, *Senior Product Manager*

Editorial, Design, and Production by Plan B Book Packagers

Captions
Cover: Perfectly suited to its Arctic habitat, the snow white snowy owl has thick plumage and feathered feet to keep it warm.
Page 1: Some birds of prey, such as this serpent eagle, are known for their keen vision and intense stare.
Pages 2–3: A European eagle-owl swoops low over a field. Its orange eyes make it appear fierce.

The National Geographic Society is one of the world's largest nonprofit scientific and educational organizations. Founded in 1888 to "increase and diffuse geographic knowledge," the Society's mission is to inspire people to care about the planet. It reaches more than 400 million people worldwide each month through its official journal, *National Geographic,* and other magazines; National Geographic Channel; television documentaries; music; radio; films; books; DVDs; maps; exhibitions; live events; school publishing programs; interactive media; and merchandise. National Geographic has funded more than 10,000 scientific research, conservation, and exploration projects and supports an education program promoting geographic literacy.

For more information, please visit nationalgeographic.com, call 1-877-873-6846 or write to the following address:
National Geographic Society
1145 17th Street N.W.
Washington, D.C. 20036-4688 U.S.A.

Visit us online at nationalgeographic.com/books

For librarians and teachers: ngchildrensbooks.org

More for kids from National Geographic:
kids.nationalgeographic.com

For information about special discounts for bulk purchases, please contact National Geographic Books Special Sales:
ngspecsales@ngs.org

For rights or permissions inquiries, please contact National Geographic Books Subsidiary Rights:
ngbookrights@ngs.org

Paperback ISBN: 978-1-4263-1889-4
Reinforced library binding ISBN: 978-1-4263-1890-0

Printed in Malaysia
21/IVM/2 (Paperback)
21/IVM/3 (RLB)